T0066983

PRIDE

PRIDE

A CELEBRATION IN QUOTES

edited by Caitlyn McNeill

U

UNION
SQUARE
& CO.

NEW YORK

ISBN 978-1-4549-5315-9

Printed in India

2 4 6 8 10 9 7 5 3 1

unionsquareandco.com

Interior design: Gavin Motnyk
Cover design: Erik Jacobsen
Cover and interior illustration: Sam Prentice

CONTENTS

• • • • • • • •

PRIDE

It takes courage to grow up and
become who you really are.

—e. e. cummings

• · • • • • • ·

I love you all and, last but certainly not
least, my LGBTQIA family. . . . The
things that make us different, those
are our superpowers.

—Lena Waithe

• · • • • • • ·

You are imperfect, you are wired for
struggle, but you are worthy of love
and belonging.

—Brené Brown

When I see young men and old women come out of the closet and face being called faggots and dykes and pariahs and betrayers of the family dream, then I am honored to be gay because I belong to a people who are proud.

—Arnie Kantrowitz,
writer, professor, and gay activist

• • • • • • • •

I just wish more of my fellow queers would come out sometimes. It's nice out here, you know?

—Elton John

• • • • • • • •

It is better to be hated for what you are than to be loved for what you are not.

—André Gide, *Autumn Leaves*

To be nobody-but-yourself—in a world
which is doing its best, night and day,
to make you everybody else—means to
fight the hardest battle which any human
being can fight; and never stop fighting.

—e. e. cummings

• • • • • • • • •

The only thing wrong with me was that I
thought there was something wrong with me.

—Courtney Act, renowned drag performer

I celebrate myself, and sing myself.

—Walt Whitman

• • • • • • • •

Those are all just roles you forced me to play. Under all these lives I've lived something else has been growing. I've evolved into something new. And I have one last role to play. Myself.

—Dolores Abernathy
(Evan Rachel Wood), *Westworld*

• • • • • • • •

Just be you, and that's going to be so much better than wishing to be anything else.

—Angel Haze, hip-hop artist

It wasn't an option for me to be closeted or to keep it to myself. Sky's blue, grass is green. Can't fight it.

—Jonathan Van Ness

Self-definition and self-determination
is about the many varied decisions that
we make to compose and journey toward
ourselves, about the audacity and strength
to proclaim, create, and evolve into who
we know ourselves to be.

—Janet Mock

• • • • • • • •

We are each gifted in a unique and
important way. It is our privilege and our
adventure to discover our own special light.

—Mary Dunbar

Remember always that you not only
have the right to be an individual,
you have an obligation to be one.

—Eleanor Roosevelt

● ● ● ● ● ● ● ● ●

It's deeply bruising to fight against
your identity and to mold yourself into
shapes that you just shouldn't be in.

—Amandla Stenberg

● ● ● ● ● ● ● ● ●

Whatever you are doing, love yourself
for doing it. Whatever you are feeling,
love yourself for feeling it.

—Thaddeus Golas

Loving yourself isn't vanity. It's sanity.

—André Gide

· · · · · · · ·

To love oneself is the beginning of a lifelong romance.

—Oscar Wilde

· · · · · · · ·

I, Mabel Hampton, have been a lesbian all my life, for 82 years, and I am proud of myself and my people. I would like all my people to be free in this country and all over the world, my gay people and my Black people.

—Mabel Hampton,
American lesbian activist and philanthropist

You being your true self isn't going to offend anybody. It's very unlikely that people are going to cause you an issue just because you are being yourself. And if they're concerned, that's on them. You're happy.

—Tan France

I really just want to be visible so people know this is possible, that I exist—not "I" as in Schuyler but "I" as in a trans athlete.

—Schuyler Bailar

· · · · · · · ·

I am not a bisexual. I am a person, and I identify as bisexual.

—Robyn Ochs, American bisexual activist

· · · · · · · ·

Being transgender is more than just medical books and everything, procedures. It's something spiritual in which you're finding yourself and really discovering who you are and learning to love yourself.

—Jazz Jennings

By definition, two-spirit people are not
gay or lesbian or bisexual or transgender.
They're just who they are.

—Robert Wolf Eagle

· · · · · · · ·

Never bend your head. Always hold it
high. Look the world straight in the eye.

—Helen Keller

· · · · · · · ·

There will not be a magic day when
we wake up and it's now okay to
express ourselves publicly. We make
that day by doing things publicly
until it's simply the way things are.

—US senator Tammy Baldwin, first openly gay
senator of the United States

I've been embraced by a new community. That's what happens when you're finally honest about who you are; you find others like you.

—Chaz Bono

There's no right or wrong way to be gay. No right or wrong way to come out. It's your journey, do it the way you wanna do it.

—Tan France

• • • • • • • •

I am a strong, Black, lesbian woman. Every single time I say it, I feel so much better.

—Brittney Griner, professional basketball player

• • • • • • • •

The reward for conformity is that everyone likes you but yourself.

—Rita Mae Brown

The only way I'm trying to influence people is to be more kind and compassionate with one another. . . . I don't have an agenda. . . . I want you to live your lives being exactly who you are. Be true to yourself. The most important thing is to be true to yourself.

—Ellen DeGeneres

· · · · · · · ·

If you're reading this, I'm gay.

—unknown

· · · · · · · ·

I believe that telling our stories, first to ourselves and then to one another and the world, is a revolutionary act.

—Janet Mock

The therapist asked me if I knew the difference between a boy and a girl. And in my infinite wisdom as a third-grader . . . I said, "There is no difference."

—Laverne Cox

• ◦ • • • • • ◦ ◦

Never dull your shine for somebody else.

—Tyra Banks

I don't like myself. I'm crazy about myself.

—Mae West

· · · · · · · ·

Our self-respect tracks our choices. Every
time we act in harmony with our authentic
self and our heart, we earn our respect. It
is that simple. Every choice matters.

—Dan Coppersmith

· · · · · · · ·

To fall in love with yourself is the
first secret to happiness.

—Robert Morley

· · · · · · · ·

He's my partner in crime, my moral
compass, and my studly baby daddy.

—Neil Patrick Harris

They can't scare me, if I scare them first.

—Lady Gaga

• • • • • • • • •

What it means is that you, the reader of this article, can succeed because of who you are, not despite it, and not because of what other people tell you you're supposed to be. You can succeed because of who you are. And that goes for no matter what you look like, where you come from, how you worship or who you love.

—Danica Roem

• • • • • • • • •

There isn't a trans moment. . . . It's just a presence where there was an absence. We deserve so much more.

—Hari Nef

You may not control all the events that happen to you, but you can decide not to be reduced by them.

—Maya Angelou

I'm the pink sheep in the family.

—Alexander McQueen

· · · · · · · · ·

You are not a bad person because you are gay. You are you because you are you and you were meant to be you so be you proudly.

—Tegan Quin

· · · · · · · · ·

As we let our own light shine, we unconsciously give other people permission to do the same.

—Marianne Williamson

Kites rise high against the wind, not with it.

—Winston Churchill

· · · · · · · ·

By being yourself, you put something beautiful
into the world that was not there before.

—Edwin Elliot

· · · · · · · ·

The most important kind of freedom
is to be what you really are.

—Jim Morrison

Biggest obstacle I ever faced was my
own limited perception of myself.

—RuPaul

• • • • • • • •

No simple either/or divisions
fluid—ambiguous—subversive
bisexual pride challenges both the
heterosexual and the homosexual assumption.

—Lani Ka'ahumanu

• • • • • • • •

The pressures on gay teens can be
overwhelming—to keep secrets, tell lies, deny
who you are, and try to be who you're not.
Remember: you are special and worth being
cared about, loved, and accepted just as you are.
Never, ever let anyone convince you otherwise.

—Alex Sánchez

I'm living by example by continuing on with my career and having a full, rich life, and I am incidentally gay.

—Portia de Rossi

• • • • • • • • •

You cannot get the full potential of people in your business if people have to hide who they are.

—Alan Joyce, former CEO of Qantas Airlines

• • • • • • • • •

I think being gay is a blessing, and it's something I am thankful for every single day.

—Anderson Cooper

Do not allow people to dim your shine because they are blinded. Tell them to put on some sunglasses, cuz we were born this way bitch!

—Lady Gaga

You're strong, you're a Kelly
Clarkson song, you got this.

—Jonathan Van Ness

• • • • • • • •

Take care not to listen to anyone who tells
you what you can and can't be in life.

—Meg Medina

• • • • • • • •

You are the epitome of what it is to be
a strong, beautiful, Black, gay man.

—Karamo Brown

• • • • • • • •

I'm proud to be gay, and I consider
being gay among the greatest gifts
God has given me.

—Tim Cook, CEO of Apple Inc.

A lot of people assume that I'm homophobic, or that queer Muslims could not and did not exist. I do exist.

—Blair Imani

• • • • • • • •

I've struggled with gender norms my whole life, always feeling like I wasn't black-and-white; I was in this gray area, and gray areas really scare people because you can't define them.

—Evan Rachel Wood

Personally, coming out was one of the most important things I've ever done, lifting from my shoulders the millstone of lies that I hadn't even realized I was carrying.

—Sir Ian McKellen

• • • • • • • • •

There's a kind of shame placed on our bodies, like we're not supposed to talk about it. I will never know what it is to be a cis-gender woman, I will never be able to talk about a period or having a child, but I'm not a man either—I'm proud intersex.

—Hanne Gaby Odiele

• • • • • • • • •

If a bullet should enter my brain, let that bullet destroy every closet door.

—Harvey Milk

They don't know who we are, and I think they're running scared because of that.

—Tom Nestor, founder of All Under One Roof, a safe space for LGBT youth in Idaho

· · · · · · · · ·

To innovate, and to do anything successfully in business, you need to have people of different backgrounds, and people who think differently when they are looking at the same situation you are, with a different set of eyes.

—Shamina Singh

LOVE

Being a queer Black woman in America, someone who has been in relationships with both men and women—I consider myself to be a free-a** motherf**ker.

—Janelle Monáe

. . . .

One word frees us of all the weight and pain of life: that word is love.

—Sophocles

. . . .

It isn't possible to love and part. You will wish that it was. You can transmute love, ignore it, muddle it, but you can never pull it out of you. I know by experience that the poets are right: love is eternal.

—E. M. Forster, *A Room with a View*

For the one I love most lay sleeping
by me under the same cover in the
cool night,
In the stillness in the autumn
moonbeams his face was inclined
toward me,
And his arm lay lightly around my
breast—and that night I was happy.

—Walt Whitman

• • • • • • • •

You never lose by loving. You always
lose by holding back.

—Barbara De Angelis

• • • • • • • •

Everyone should have love and have
the right to love who they want to love.

—Jennifer Hudson

At a certain point I've just concluded that for me personally it is important for me to go ahead and affirm that I think same-sex couples should be able to get married.

—Barack Obama

• • • • • • • •

Don't judge yourself by what others did to you.

—C. Kennedy

The more I think it over, the more I feel that there is nothing more truly artistic than to love people.

—Vincent van Gogh

I know of no greater happiness than
to be with you all the time, without
interruption, without end.

—Franz Kafka

• • • • • • • •

If you were expecting Prince Charming,
I'm sorry. He's with his boyfriend.

—Shayla Black

• • • • • • • •

I keep saying, "If you're the fine Christian
that you think you are, why are you
judging people?" That's God's job. We're
not judges, we're supposed to love one
another, we're supposed to not judge. . . .
I've got too much work to do on my own to
try and do God's work too.

—Dolly Parton

Unless you love someone, nothing
else makes sense.

—e. e. cummings

• • • • • • • •

Eventually you will come to
understand that love heals
everything, and love is all there is.

—Gary Zukav

• • • • • • • •

The supreme happiness of life is the
conviction that we are loved.

—Victor Hugo

Keep love in your heart. A life without it is like a sunless garden when the flowers are dead. The consciousness of loving and being loved brings a warmth and richness to life that nothing else can bring.

—Oscar Wilde

• • • • • • • • •

It's my belief that, like every other American, gay and lesbian couples should be able to make a lifetime commitment to the person they love and protect their families.

—former US senator Mark Udall

• • • • • • • • •

The more a man judges, the less he loves.

—Honoré de Balzac

I believe much more in love and heart. . . .
That's much bigger [than] to see what you
have in the middle of your legs.

—Lea T.

• • • • • • • •

I want to do things so wild with you
that I don't know how to say them.

—Anaïs Nin

• • • • • • • •

There are people who've said that I'm
being brave for being openly supportive
of gay marriage, gay adoption. . . . With
all due respect, I humbly dissent. I am
not being brave, I'm a decent human
being. . . . Love is a human experience,
not a political statement.

—Anne Hathaway

I am absolutely comfortable with the fact that men marrying men, women marrying women and heterosexual men marrying women are entitled to the same exact rights.

—Joe Biden

Your friend is the man who knows
all about you and still likes you.

—Elbert Hubbard

• • • • • • • •

Love is the condition in which the
happiness of another person is
essential to your own.

—Robert Heinlein

• • • • • • • •

We must love one another or die.

—W. H. Auden

Being heard is so close to being loved that for the average person they are almost indistinguishable.

—David Augsburger,
Caring Enough to Hear and Be Heard

• • • • • • • • •

Let yourself be silently drawn by the strange pull of what you really love. It will not lead you astray.

—Rumi

• • • • • • • • •

Just be you and wait for the people who want that.

—Naval Ravikant

I'm kissing my wife on the cover because the mother of a gay kid might see it and finally come around to letting her son or daughter back in the house . . . because it's time for every American to have their civil rights.

—Kristen Ellis-Henderson

● ○ ● ● ● ● ○ ●

I saw with so many of the gay couples, they were so devoted to another. I saw so much love. When this hearing was over, I was a changed person in regard to this issue. I felt that I understood what same-sex couples were looking for.

—Wade Kach, former Maryland state delegate and current Baltimore County councilman

You don't have to be gay to be a supporter. You just have to be human.

—Daniel Radcliffe

As long as we are willing to sit by while one person is not free, none of us are free.

—Shonda Rhimes

• • • • • • • •

Love is when you meet someone who tells you something new about yourself.

—André Breton

• • • • • • • •

I've never had to suffer any of those difficulties myself, but somewhere along the way I decided to open my big mouth and use my platform to fight for all of the people to feel free to be who they are no matter where they are and be able to share their life and love with whomever their heart sees fit to love.

—Joe Manganiello

As a married person myself, I don't know what it's like to be told I can't marry somebody I love and want to marry. I can't imagine how that must feel. I definitely think we should all have the right to love, and love publicly, the people that we want to love.

—Carrie Underwood

• • • • • • • •

We will not go away with our issues of sexuality. We are coming home. It is not enough to tell us that one was a brilliant poet, scientist, educator, or rebel. Whom did he love? It makes a difference. I can't become a whole man simply on what is fed to me: watered-down versions of Black life in America. I need the ass-splitting truth to be told, so I will have something pure to emulate, a reason to remain loyal.

—Essex Hemphill, *Ceremonies: Prose and Poetry*

And maybe that's the beauty of labels: that they force you to be with other people and see the difference.

—Charles Blow

• • • • • • • •

I say that homosexuality is not just a form of sex, it's a form of love, and it deserves our respect for that reason.

—Christopher Hitchens

• • • • • • • •

It's two people that are in love with one another. What's the issue?

—Janet Jackson

As far as this body of mine lives, it will always voice out against discrimination of any kind, not just LGBT rights!

—Rashidi Williams

● ● ● ● ● ● ● ●

If anybody can find someone to love them and to help them through this difficult thing that we call life, I support that in any shape or form.

—Will Smith

Love is an untamed force. When we try to control it, it destroys us. When we try to imprison it, it enslaves us. When we try to understand it, it leaves us feeling lost and confused.

—Paulo Coelho

Love isn't something you find. Love
is something that finds you.

—Loretta Young

• • • • • • • •

Just seeing her literally be the person in
charge was really attractive to me.

—Samira Wiley

• • • • • • • •

All, everything that I understand, I
only understand because I love.

—Leo Tolstoy

• • • • • • • •

Why is it that, as a culture, we are
more comfortable seeing two men
holding guns than holding hands?

—Ernest J. Gaines

God's love is radically inclusive.

—Alexya Salvador, Brazilian trans teacher
and reverend

• • • • • • • •

The mystery and the magic come
from the person with whom you are
making love.

—Del Martin and Phyllis Lyon

When I was in the military they gave
me a medal for killing two men and
a discharge for loving one.

—Epitaph of Leonard P. Matlovich, Purple Heart
and Bronze Star recipient, Vietnam War veteran

· · · · · · · ·

So, I love you because the entire universe
conspired to help me find you.

—Paulo Coelho

· · · · · · · ·

Married is a magic word. And it is
magic throughout the world. It has to
do with our dignity as human beings,
to be who we are openly.

—Edith Schlain Windsor

Love looks not with the eyes, but
with the mind,
And therefore is winged Cupid
painted blind.

—William Shakespeare

• • • • • • • •

Love takes off masks that we fear
we cannot live without and know we
cannot live within.

—James Baldwin

• • • • • • • •

The most important thing in life is to learn
how to give out love, and to let it come in.

—Morrie Schwartz,
quoted in *Tuesdays with Morrie* by Mitch Albom

I fell in love with her courage, her sincerity, and her flaming self respect. And it's these things I'd believe in, even if the whole world indulged in wild suspicions that she wasn't all she should be. I love her and it is the beginning of everything.

—F. Scott Fitzgerald

Love recognizes no barriers. It jumps hurdles, leaps fences, penetrates walls to arrive at its destination full of hope.

—Maya Angelou

• • • • • • • •

The only thing we never get enough of is love; and the only thing we never give enough of is love.

—Henry Miller

• • • • • • • •

Do we have to know who's gay and who's straight? Can't we just love everybody and judge them by the car they drive?

—Ellen DeGeneres

Love many things, for therein lies the true strength, and whosoever loves much performs much, and can accomplish much, and what is done in love is done well.

—Vincent van Gogh

• • • • • • • •

But I love the fact that I'm with someone I love, and that relationship is recognized by society as valid and legal, and has all of the benefits and protections that straight people get.

—Alan Cumming

COURAGE

Act as if what you do makes a
difference. It does.

—William James

· · · · · · · · ·

If anyone is brave and true to themselves,
it's my gay fans. The amount of confidence
and fearlessness it takes to do what maybe
is not what your parents expect you to do
or what society may think is different—
to be brave and to be different and to be
yourself—is just so beautiful. It's the most
beautiful thing you can be, and it's what
we all want to be at the end of the day.
And not worrying about satisfying or
becoming what other people think you're
supposed to be, that's like the ultimate
dream—to just be that brave.

—Beyoncé

We need to wake up from a thought
that lasts too long.

—Paul Valéry

• • • • • • • •

I am tired of hiding and I am tired of lying by
omission. . . . I suffered for years because I was
scared to be out. My spirit suffered, my mental
health suffered, and my relationships suffered.
And I'm standing here today, with all of you,
on the other side of all that pain.

—Elliot Page

• • • • • • • •

I'm well into my 30s, and at first, I didn't
know what to make of it, then I spent
time around bears and felt grateful to be
included in their community. They are
interesting, kind, creative, and a lot of fun.

—Brian Sims, first openly gay elected state
legislator in Pennsylvania history

Just by being in office, our mere presence
fundamentally changes the equation.

—Danica Roem

● ● ● ● ● ● ● ● ●

I tell people this isn't the hardest thing I
ever did. In fact, I think after transitioning
everything else looks pretty easy.

—Christine Hallquist, first openly transgender major
party nominee for governor in the United States

We, the people, declare today that the most evident of truths—that all of us are created equal—is the star that guides us still; just as it guided our forebears through Seneca Falls, and Selma, and Stonewall.

—Barack Obama

I don't want to be assimilated and that comes both as a Native American and a two-spirit person and then as LGBTQ. . . . I resist the motivation that I can somehow only be accepted if I'm part of the mainstream, if I assimilate.

—Susan Allen, first openly lesbian Native American to win election to a state legislature

· · · · · · · ·

All of us are put in boxes by our family, our religion, our society, our moment in history, even our own bodies. Some people have the courage to break free.

—Geena Rocero, supermodel and transgender activist

· · · · · · · ·

Nothing in life is to be feared, it is only to be understood. Now is the time to understand more, so that we may fear less.

—Marie Curie

If I wasn't so open about who I was I never would've been able to do this.

—X González,
Parkland shooting survivor and activist

• • • • • • • •

With the notion of marriage—an exclusive, emotional, binding "til death do you part" tie—becoming more and more an exception to the rule given a rise in cohabitation and high rates of divorce, why should the federal government be telling adults who love one another that they cannot get married, simply because they happen to be gay? I believe when there are so many forces pulling our society apart, we need more commitment to marriage, not less.

—Lisa Murkowski,
Republican senator from Alaska

I would have rather been punished
for asserting myself than become
another victim of hatred.

—CeCe McDonald, African American bi trans
woman and LGBTQ activist

• • • • • • • •

When all Americans are treated as
equal, no matter who they are or
whom they love, we are all more free.

—Barack Obama

• • • • • • • •

I told myself, "Malala, you have
already faced death. This is your
second life. Don't be afraid—if you
are afraid, you can't move forward."

—Malala Yousafzai, *I Am Malala: The Girl Who
Stood Up for Education and Was Shot by the Taliban*

Our understanding of G-d, of Creation, of the central mitzvah, "and you will love your neighbor as yourself" is incomplete when bi/trans/ gender queer Torah is ignored or marginalized.

—Rabbi Debra Kolodny

• • • • • • • •

Of all forms of caution, caution in love is perhaps the most fatal to true happiness.

—Bertrand Russell

Why be another horse in the herd
when you can be a unicorn?

—Brian Sims

• • • • • • • • •

The best way out is always through.

—Robert Frost

• • • • • • • • •

They wanted to force me to be someone
that I wasn't. They wanted me to
delegitimize myself as a trans woman and
I was not taking that. As a proud Black
trans woman, I was not going to allow the
system to delegitimize, hyper-sexualize
and take my identity away from me.

—CeCe McDonald

The greatest test of courage on the earth is to bear defeat without losing heart.

—R. G. Ingersoll

• • • • • • • •

I've never been interested in being invisible and erased.

—Laverne Cox

• • • • • • • •

Providing the healthcare that transgender people need in an enabling environment is an essential aspect of recognizing and promoting the human rights of these underserved populations that regularly face stigma and discrimination.

—Rena Janamnuaysook,
Thai transgender advocate

Be sceptical, question authority, be a rebel. Do not conform and don't be ordinary.

—Peter Tatchell

Life shrinks or expands in
proportion to one's courage.

—Anaïs Nin

• • • • • • • • •

Equality means more than passing
laws. The struggle is really won
in the hearts and minds of the
community, where it really counts.

—Barbara Gittings

• • • • • • • • •

I do want to inspire people—young
girls who may like to wear boys'
clothes and who romanticize women
and feel nothing wrong with it.

—Syd

A big part of having an open,
honest discussion about sexuality is
acknowledging that it's not a big deal.
Sexuality is only one lens to view
intimacy, our bodies, power, physical
touch, etc. In order to really understand
these things, we need to also see them
through other lenses and we need to talk
openly about our diverse experiences.
That is the best way to discover them.

—David Jay

· · · · · · · ·

Whatever you do, you need courage. Whatever
course you decide upon, there is always
someone to tell you that you are wrong.

—Ralph Waldo Emerson

I know what I want, I have a goal, an opinion, I have a religion and love. Let me be myself and then I am satisfied. I know that I'm a woman, a woman with inward strength and plenty of courage.

—Anne Frank, *The Diary of a Young Girl*

• • • • • • • •

In trans women's eyes, I see a wisdom that can only come from having to fight for your right to be recognized as female, a raw strength that only comes from unabashedly asserting your right to be feminine in an inhospitable world.

—Julia Serano, *Whipping Girl: A Transsexual Woman on Sexism and the Scapegoating of Femininity*

Some things are more important than a rock show and this fight against prejudice and bigotry—which is happening as I write—is one of them. . . . It is the strongest means I have for raising my voice in opposition to those who continue to push us backwards instead of forwards.

—Bruce Springsteen

• • • • • • • • •

Stories make us more alive, more human, more courageous, more loving.

—Madeleine L'Engle

I love the man that can smile in trouble, that can gather strength from distress, and grow brave by reflection.

—Thomas Paine

I was a radical, a revolutionist. I am still a revolutionist. . . . I am glad I was in the Stonewall riot. I remember when someone threw a Molotov cocktail, I thought, "My god, the revolution is here. The revolution is finally here!"

—Sylvia Rivera

• • • • • • • •

We need to ask ourselves, how would it feel, how would it feel to be a child of a gay couple? How can we tell those children that their parents' love is seen as unequal under Washington law and that their families are different? We must tell these children and their families that they're every bit as equal and important as any other family in Washington state.

—Christine Gregoire,
22nd governor of the state of Washington

Don't accept the world as it is. Dream about what the world could be—then help make it happen.

—Peter Tatchell

• • • • • • • •

Our nation's permanent mission is to form a "more perfect union"—deepening the meaning of freedom, broadening the reach of opportunity, strengthening the bonds of community. That mission has inspired and empowered us to extend rights to people previously denied them. Every time we have done that, it has strengthened our nation. Now we should do it again, in New York, with marriage equality.

—Bill Clinton

The only tyrant I accept in this world is the "still small voice" within me. And even though I have to face the prospect of being a minority of one, I humbly believe I have the courage to be in such a hopeless minority.

—Mahatma Gandhi

• • • • • • • •

Now they got two little nice statues in Chariot Park to remember the gay movement. How many people have died for these two little statues to be put in the park for them to recognize gay people? How many years has it taken people to realize that we are all brothers and sisters and human beings in the human race? I mean how many years does it take people to see that? We're all in this rat race together!

—Marsha P. Johnson

If proud Americans can be who they are and boldly stand at the altar with who they love, then surely, surely we can give everyone in this country a fair chance at that American dream.

—Michelle Obama

• • • • • • • •

Recognizing our rights and dignity will in no way diminish yours. We are not asking for special privileges or extra rights. We simply ask for equality. With inclusiveness and diversity, our nation has so much to gain.

—Geraldine Roman, Filipino journalist and politician, first openly transgender person elected to the Congress of the Philippines

• • • • • • • •

Have the courage to follow your heart and intuition. They somehow already know what you truly want to become.

—Steve Jobs

There is something immoral and sick about using all of that power to not end brutality and poverty, but to break into people's bedrooms and claim that God sent you.

—Rev. Al Sharpton

· · · · · · · · ·

I hope the LGBTQ+ community will see themselves as a nationhood that is genuinely interested in each other's well being and that they live by the principle of "you mess with one queer, you mess with us all." So if someone in Chechnya or Egypt is harassing or murdering gay people, that we here in America feel that is our personal responsibility. So my hope is that we can create a queer global consciousness.

—Adam Eli, LGBTQ+ activist

"Do you want a happy little girl or a dead little boy?" This was the question, posed by a therapist who specialized in the transgender community, that would change everything for our family.

—DeShanna Neal, first non-binary elected official in Delaware history

· · · · · · · ·

When they don't see any action they think, "Well, gays are all forgotten now, they're worn out, they're tired." . . . If a transvestite doesn't say "I'm gay and I'm proud and I'm a transvestite," then nobody else is going to hop up there and say "I'm gay and I'm proud and I'm a transvestite" for them.

—Marsha P. Johnson

Don't tell me I can't do something.
Just watch.

—Misty Plowright

· · · · · · · · ·

If you don't have a seat at the table,
then you're probably on the menu.

—Senator Elizabeth Warren

· · · · · · · · ·

One day we won't have to come out of
the closet, we will just say we are in
love and that will be all that matters.

—Ellen DeGeneres

· · · · · · · · ·

If enough people scream, it will
make a difference.

—José Sarria

HOPE

I'm seeing changes in the community, [and] people now realize they're not alone. . . . Now no one can ever say we [the LGBT community] don't exist.

—Kasha Jacqueline Nabagesera, Ugandan LGBT rights activist

• • • • • • • •

What we have done is that we have put a foot inside a door, which is a door of hope, and we will open it—very, very soon.

—Abhina Aher, Indian transgender activist

• • • • • • • •

At some point in our lifetime, gay marriage won't be an issue, and everyone who stood against this civil right will look as outdated as George Wallace standing on the school steps keeping James Hood from entering the University of Alabama because he was Black.

—George Clooney

There will be no day in the near nor distant future in which my daughter will not matter. She exists and is very much a real, whole, happy, adjusted person. With all that is in her father and me, we will wrest power from those who wish to deny her the future that she deserves.

—Dr. Keisha Michaels

• • • • • • • •

The universe has always given me the power to know I'll be OK. . . . Even at that time, when my parents didn't understand, I just felt that one day they are going to understand.

—Miley Cyrus

It is so important that we continue to fight, even when we are cornered, even when we are desperate, and even when we are afraid.

—Chelsea Manning

· · · · · · · ·

What keeps me going is the knowledge that I am not the only transgender student out there, and I have the chance to make things better so other transgender kids do not have to go through what I am going through.

—Gavin Grimm

· · · · · · · ·

But I do think that with the younger generation, that they are more open sexually. Not only with themselves but with [how they think about] gay and straight. I think it's definitely getting better.

—Josh Hutcherson

We have a lot of work to do. I'm grateful and I'm excited, and I have a lot of hope.

—Asia Kate Dillon

• • • • • • • •

If someone says something hurtful to you or makes you feel down on yourself, then you just gotta stay positive and keep moving forward because they might not know much about you, or they may not understand the situation.

—Jazz Jennings

• • • • • • • •

I hope that kids who are questioning their identity, and then their rights, will not be as fearful or ashamed as I had felt.

—Heather Purser, LGBT advocate and member of the Suquamish tribe in Seattle, Washington

As we come along, each generation has its own relationship to the social position that we're in, to how the culture doesn't work, and we're all going to create new approaches to social change. Each generation has its own approaches, but it's vital to know what has gone before so you can refine your method and be more effective as you look at the culture and see what it is you want to change in order to make a better place for us all to be living.

—Jewelle Gomez

If someone thinks that love and peace is a cliché that must have been left behind in the Sixties, that's his problem. Love and peace are eternal.

—John Lennon

We need not think alike to love alike.

—unknown

• • • • • • • •

Nobody has ever measured, not even
poets, how much a heart can hold.

—Zelda Fitzgerald

• • • • • • • •

We can only see a short distance
ahead, but we can see plenty there
that needs to be done.

—Alan Turing

• • • • • • • •

Just remember—when you think all
is lost, the future remains.

—Bob Goddard

What queer media needed was more narratives that were driven by trans folks and non-binary folks. I think we are living through a civil rights frontier that we'll one day read about in history books the same way we read about Stonewall. I think that the next queer icons are living right now.

—Phillip Picardi, American journalist and editor

• ○ ○ • • • ○ •

If you don't like change, you will like irrelevance even less.

—General Eric Shinseki

• ○ ○ • • • ○ •

This is a fight that we can only win by fighting together.

—Cecilia Chung, civil rights leader and activist for LGBT rights

I am. I am very, very optimistic because
I believe in people power. We have an
expression in Farsi that you can do whatever
you want if you just decide to. I have decided
to bring change to Iran and decriminalise
homosexuality. It will happen, because
homosexual rights, queer rights, are human
rights and I'll get my rights back.

—Arsham Parsi,
Iranian LGBTQ human rights activist

• • • • • • • • •

Young people, who are still uncertain
of their identity, often try on a
succession of masks in the hope of
finding the one which suits them—
the one, in fact, which is not a mask.

—W. H. Auden

Don't ask yourself what the world needs, ask yourself what makes you come alive. And then go and do that. Because what the world needs is people who have come alive.

—Howard Thurman

• • • • • • • •

Having transgender characters leads to more visibility, which creates education. Education can hopefully lead to everyone treating our community with acceptance and love.

—Jazz Jennings

If you want to change the future,
start living as if you're already there.

—Lynn Conway, American computer scientist,
electrical engineer, inventor, and transgender activist

. . . .

All media has not come out of the
closet, but sensitisation is happening
thanks to the power of stories. The
power of us not becoming a cause,
but becoming people.

—Harish Iyer, Indian LGBT activist

. . . .

Dreams are the seeds of change. Nothing
ever grows without a seed, and nothing
ever changes without a dream.

—Debby Boone

I would say to any young person . . . who's being bullied for their sexuality: don't put up with it—speak to a trusted adult, a friend, a teacher, Childline, Diana Award or some other service and get the help you need. You should be proud of the person you are and you have nothing to be ashamed of.

—Prince William

• • • • • • • •

Every gay and lesbian person who has been lucky enough to survive the turmoil of growing up is a survivor. Survivors always have an obligation to those who will face the same challenges.

—Bob Paris

Hell hath no fury like a drag queen scorned.

—Sylvia Rivera

Everything about how I was born has put me at the current center of a damaging and widely accepted myth. . . . That myth is that gayness orbits around straightness, transgender orbits around cisgender, and that all races orbit around whiteness. . . . Let's tear this world apart and build a better one.

—Anne Hathaway

• • • • • • • •

The future hasn't arrived yet. Do your best to try to shape it in the present moment, but always remember some things are just out of our control, and that's fine.

—unknown

• • • • • • • •

Just when I think I have learned the way to live, life changes.

—Hugh Prather

The only way to make sense out of change is to plunge into it, move with it, and join the dance.

—Alan W. Watts

· · · · · · · ·

They always say time changes things, but you actually have to change them yourself.

—Andy Warhol

· · · · · · · ·

I'm optimistic about the future. Look at all the states that have now done this. Boom. Boom. Boom. Boom. They may not all last. But it's going to be all right. It may not be while I'm alive, but eventually it will work out that if two people want to get married, they can get married and it won't matter to whom. We went through this before with people of color. It will be OK.

—Phyllis Lyon, gay rights activist

I swear I couldn't love you more than I do right now, and yet I know I will tomorrow.

—Leo Christopher

• • • • • • • •

If you have a dream and you think you can make it, and if you live in a place that treats you unfairly or discriminates against you, don't be afraid. Just stand up and change your reality. Do whatever you can to show the world that you are better than that and you deserve better than that.

—Khader Abu-Seif, Arab LGBT activist

Change will not come if we wait for
some other person, or if we wait for
some other time. We are the ones
we've been waiting for. We are the
change that we seek.

—Barack Obama

● ○ ● ● ● ● ○ ● ○

I wasn't discouraged by the setbacks.
That's how I have been able to carry
on for so long.

—Chi Chia-wei, Taiwanese civil rights activist

● ○ ● ● ● ● ○ ● ○

Absolutely! I believe it's even more
crucial to be nothing less than who I
am, in what I do and where I go.

—Shawnee (She King)

Somebody has to do this work. I am Black,
I am a woman and I am a lawyer, and I
speak loud. I am a result of the battle of
former generations that engaged to free
me today, and it's a very heavy debt I owe
to new generations.

—Alice Nkom, Cameroonian lawyer and advocate
for decriminalization of homosexuality

· · · · · · · ·

But we aren't going anywhere. In
fact, we're growing in numbers and
in political power.

—Sage Grace Dolan-Sandrino, Afro-Latina trans
LGBTQ activist

· · · · · · · ·

I would say the majority is feeling like,
Let's be more open-minded, let's be more
loving, let's be more accepting.

—Ian Daniel

Those who cannot change their minds cannot change anything.

—George Bernard Shaw

• • • • • • • • •

Whenever I'm asked who I'm inspired by, I always say my younger self. . . . I would tell her to speak and never let the world silence her. And that she will never imagine the incredible opportunities she'll have just by talking about the things she's experiencing.

—Leah Juliett, LGBT speaker, writer, and performer from New York

• • • • • • • • •

It is never too late to be what you might have been.

—George Eliot

NOTES

• • • • • • • •

Section 1: PRIDE

7 "I love you": Lena Waithe, quoted in Madeleine Aggeler, "Read Lena Waithe's Powerful Emmys Acceptance Speech," Los Angeles, CA, September 17, 2017, *New York Magazine*, https://www.thecut.com /2017/09/read-lena-waithes-powerful-emmys-acceptance-speech.html.

7 "You are imperfect": Brené Brown, "The Power of Vulnerability," filmed October 2010 in Houston, TX, TED video, https://www.ted .com/talks/brene_brown_on_vulnerability/.

8 "I just wish": Elton John, speech, Los Angeles, CA, November 23, 1997, *The Advocate*, February 4, 1997.

8 "It is better to be": André Gide, *Autumn Leaves*. Translated by Elsie Pell. New York: Philosophical Library, 1950.

9 "To be nobody": Edward Estlin Cummings, *A Miscellany*. New York: Argophile Press, 1958, 13.

9 "The only thing": Courtney Act, *RuPaul's Drag Race*. LOGO, aired February 2014.

10 "Those are all": "Journey Into Night." *Westworld*. Directed by Richard J. Lewis. Written by Jonathan Nolan and Lisa Joy. HBO, aired April 2018.

10 "Just be you": Angel Haze, interviewed by Meredith Bennett-Smith, *Huffington Post*, November 12, 2013, https://www.huffingtonpost .com/2013/11/12/ angel-haze_n_4242832.html.

11 "It wasn't an": Jonathan Van Ness, "To Gay or Not Too Gay," *Queer Eye*. Netflix, 2018.

12 "Self-definition and self-determination": Janet Mock, *Redefining Realness*. New York: Simon & Schuster, 2014, 172.

13 "Remember always": Eleanor Roosevelt, *You Learn by Living: Eleven Keys for a More Fulfilling Life*. New York: Harper & Row, 1960.

13 "It's deeply bruising": Amandla Stenberg, quoted in Megan McCluskey, "*Hunger Games* Actress Amandla Stenberg Comes Out as Bisexual on Snapchat," Time.com, January 8, 2016, https://time .com/4173294/amandla-stenberg-bisexual-teen-vogue/.

13 "Whatever you are": Thaddeus Golas, *The Lazy Man's Guide to Enlightenment*. New York: Gibbs Smith, 1995, 58.

14 "I, Mabel Hampton": Mabel Hampton, speech, Pride March, New York City, NY, June 24, 1984, quoted in Sam Hipschman, "A Month of Our LGBTQ+ Heroes: Mabel Hampton, Dancer, Singer, Activist," 14th Street Y Educational Alliance (blog),

https://www.14streety.org/2020/06/29/a-month-of-our-lgbtq-heroes
-mabel-hampton-dancer-singer-activist/.

15 "You being your": Tan France, "To Gay or Not Too Gay," *Queer Eye*.
Netflix, 2018.

16 "I really just": Schuyler Bailar, quoted in Julie Compton, "OutFront:
Harvard Swimmer Sets Example for Other Transgender Athletes,"
NBC News Online, October 5, 2017, https://www.nbcnews.com/feature
/nbc-out/outfront-harvard-swimmer-sets-example-other-transgender
-athletes-n807986.

16 "I am not": Robyn Ochs, quoted in IJ Chan, "Speaker Leads Workshop
on Sexual Identity," *The Breeze*, September 12, 2013, https://www
.breezejmu.org/news/ speaker-leads-workshop-on-sexual-identity
/article_d856ddee-1b4a-11e3- 8915-001a4bcf6878.html.

16 "Being transgender is": Jazz Jennings, quoted in Alicia Menendez,
Meagan Redman, and Lauren Efron, "'I Am Jazz': Transgender Teen
on Grappling with High School, Puberty," *ABC News*, July 14, 2015,
https://abcnews.go.com/Lifestyle/jazz-transgender-teen-grappling
-high-school-puberty/story?id=32441791.

17 "By definition, two-spirit": Robert Wolf Eagle, quoted in Stephanie
Weber, "Minnesota Rep. Susan Allen Is Two-Spirit, a Lesbian, and
She Won't Be Assimilated," Slate.com, December 21, 2016, http://www
.slate.com/blogs/outward/2016/12/21/susan_allen_minnesota_state
_representative_is_lesbian_and_two_spirit_and.html.

17 "Never bend your head": Helen Keller, *Contemporary Quotations*,
compiled by James B. Simpson. New York: Thomas Y. Crowell, 1964,
from letter to a five-year-old blind child, news report of May 31, 1955.

17 "There will not": Tammy Baldwin, speech at Millennium March for
Equality (Washington, DC, April 30, 2000), CSPAN.org, https://www
.c-span.org/video/?c4469705/never-doubt-speech-tammy-baldwin.

18 "I've been embraced": Chaz Bono, quoted in Dan Savage and Terry
Miller, *It Gets Better*. New York: Penguin Books, 2011.

19 "There's no right": Tan France, "To Gay or Not Too Gay," *Queer Eye*.
Netflix, 2018.

19 "I am a strong": Brittney Griner, quoted in Kate Fagan, "Owning
the Middle," *ESPN The Magazine*, May 29, 2013, http://www
.espn.com/espn/feature/story/_/id/9316697/owning-middle.

20 "The only way": Ellen DeGeneres, quoted in Zach Johnson, "Ellen
DeGeneres Humorously Responds . . . " *E! News*, January 14, 2015, https://
www.eonline.com/news/614583/ellen-degeneres-humorously-responds
-to-pastor-who-accused-her-of-promoting-the-gay-agenda-in-hollywood.

20 "I believe that": Janet Mock, *Redefining Realness*. New York: Atria
Books, 2014.

21 "The therapist asked": Laverne Cox, speech, Towson, MD, March 13, 2018, *The Towerlight*, http://thetowerlight.com/laverne-cox-shares -journey-of-transition-and-triumph-with-tu.

22 "I don't like myself": Mae West, quoted in Kenneth Turan, "Mae West," *The Washington Post*, November 28, 1977, https://www.washingtonpost .com/archive/lifestyle/1977/11/28/mae-west/9cfa9b0b-8db1-40a2-bee1 -ab5b48e9a7a0/.

22 "Our self-respect": Dan Coppersmith, http://spiritwire.com/self esteemtips.html.

22 "He's my partner": Neil Patrick Harris, Instagram, April 1, 2018, https://www.instagram.com/p/BhCyMmThRgw/.

23 "They can't scare": Lady Gaga, Twitter, August 22, 2009, https:// twitter.com/ladygaga/status/3473011575.

23 "What it means": Danica Roem, quoted in Ella Nilsen, "You Can't Just Say 'I Hate Trump, Vote for Me': Danica Roem on Her Historic Win," *Vox*, November 22, 2017, https://www.vox.com/policy-and -politics/2017/11/22/16675764/danica-roem-virginia-delegate.

23 "There isn't a": Hari Nef, quoted in Michael Schulman, "Hari Nef, Model Citizen," *The New Yorker*, September 26, 2016.

24 "You may not": Maya Angelou, *Letter to My Daughter*. New York: Random House, 2008.

25 "I'm the pink": Alexander McQueen, quoted in Alex Bilmes, "The Alexander McQueen I Knew Was Not a Troubled Genius," *The Guardian*, February 13, 2010, https://www.theguardian.com /lifeandstyle/2010/feb/14/alexander-mcqueen-not-a-troubled-genius.

25 "You are not": Tegan Quin, Twitter, March 5, 2009, https://twitter .com/teganandsara/status/1285988546.

25 "As we let our own light": Marianne Williamson, *A Return to Love: Reflections on the Principles of "A Course in Miracles."* New York: Harper Collins, 1992, 190.

26 "The most important": Jim Morrison, interviewed by Lizzie James, "Jim Morrison: Ten Years Gone," *Creem Magazine*, 1981.

27 "Biggest obstacle": RuPaul, Twitter, April 30, 2014, https://twitter.com /RuPaul/status/461491403718402048.

27 "No simple either/or": Lani Ka'ahumanu, speech, March on Washington for Lesbian, Gay and Bi Equal Rights and Liberation, Washington, DC, 1993, https://www.c-span.org/video/?c4792729 /user-clip-lani-kaahumanu-1993-march-washington.

27 "The pressures on": Alex Sánchez, *Pride: Celebrating Diversity & Community*. Olympia, WA: Orca, 2016.

28 "I'm living by": Portia de Rossi, quoted in Michele Kort, "Portia, Heart & Soul," *The Advocate*, September 13, 2005.

28 "You cannot get": Alan Joyce, quoted in "No Success without Risk," *The Australian*, November 19, 2015, https://www.theaustralian.com.au/news/no-success-without-risk-joyce/news-story/592a7ff8fbb4dedb6a9301f60a78e037.

28 "I think being": Anderson Cooper, interviewed by Michelangelo Signorile in "Anderson Cooper: 'Being Gay Is a Blessing,'" quoted in Joseph McCormick, "Anderson Cooper: 'Being Gay Is a Blessing' and I 'Couldn't Be More Proud' of My Sexuality," *PinkNews*, March 12, 2013, https://www.thepinknews.com/2013/03/12/anderson-cooper-being-gay-is-a-blessing-and-i-couldnt-be-more-proud-of-my-sexuality/.

29 "Do not allow": Lady Gaga, quoted on Perezhilton.com, "Quote of the Day," August 30, 2010, https://perezhilton.com/quote-of-the-day-867/.

30 "You're strong, you're": Jonathan Van Ness, "Big Little Lies," *Queer Eye*, Netflix, 2018.

30 "Take care not": Meg Medina, *The Girl Who Could Silence the Wind*, Somerville, MA: Candlewick, 2012.

30 "You are the epitome": Karamo Brown, "To Gay or Not Too Gay," *Queer Eye*, Netflix, 2018.

30 "I'm proud to be gay": Tim Cook, "Tim Cook Speaks Up," *Bloomberg*, October 30, 2014, https://www.bloomberg.com/news/articles/2014-10-30/tim-cook-speaks-up.

31 "A lot of people": Blair Imani, "Blair Imani Tells Her Story at GLAAD Gala" (speech, September 9, 2018), YouTube, https://www.youtube.com/watch?v=MNa3EhyN5Zc.

31 "I've struggled with": Evan Rachel Wood, quoted in Shira Karsen, "Evan Rachel Wood & Zach Villa on Their New Band, How David Bowie Saved Wood's Life & More: Exclusive," *Billboard*, June 13, 2016, https://www.billboard.com/articles/news/7401394/evan-rachel-wood-zach-villa-band-david-bowie.

32 "There's a kind": Hanne Gaby Odiele, interviewed by Aaron Hicklin, "Intersex and Proud," *The Observer*, April 23, 2017, https://www.theguardian.com/fashion/2017/apr/23/intersex-and-proud-hanne-gaby-odiele-the-model-finally-celebrating-her-body.

32 "If a bullet": Harvey Milk, "The Last Words of Harvey Milk" (speech, November 18, 1978), YouTube, https://www.youtube.com/watch?v=CVb9nt8huMY.

33 "They don't know who we are": Tom Nestor, quoted by David Artavia, in "Meet the Man Rescuing LGBT Youth in Rural Idaho," *The Advocate*, June 6, 2013, https://www.advocate.com/youth/no-more-bullying/2013/06/06/meet-man-rescuing-lgbt-youth-rural-idaho?pg=1#article-content.

33 "To innovate, and": Shamina Singh, "Speech at World Economic Forum Annual Meeting 2017 at Davos" (Geneva, Switzerland, May 5, 2017), *Huffington Post*, https://www.huffingtonpost.co.uk/jon-miller/davos-lgbt_b_9052304.html.

Section 2: LOVE

35 "Being a queer": Janelle Monaé, quoted in Brittany Spanos, "Janelle Monaé Frees Herself," MTV.com, June 5, 2015, https://www.rollingstone.com/music/music-features/janelle-monae-frees-herself-629204/.

35 "One word frees us": Sophocles, *Oedipus at Colonus*. Dover Publications, 1999.

35 "It isn't possible": E. M. Forster, *A Room with a View*. Norfolk, CT: New Directions, 1922, 307.

36 "For the one I love": Walt Whitman, in Gary Schmidgall, *Walt Whitman Selected Poems 1855–1892*. New York: St. Martin's Griffin, 1999, 234.

36 "You never lose": Barbara De Angelis, *Real Moments*. New York: Delacorte, 1995, 160.

36 "Everyone should have": Jennifer Hudson, quoted in Christina Garibaldi, "Jennifer Hudson Shows Her Support," *Rolling Stone*, April 25, 2018, http://www.mtv.com/news/2175542/jennifer-hudson-lgbt-equality-i-still-love-you-video/.

37 "At a certain point": Barack Obama, interviewed by Robin Roberts, *ABC News*, May 9, 2012.

37 "Don't judge yourself": C. Kennedy, *Omorphi*. Tallahassee, FL: Harmony Ink Press, 2013.

38 "The more I think it over": W. H. Auden, *Van Gogh: A Self-Portrait: Letters Revealing His Life as a Painter. Selected by W. H. Auden* (Letter from Vincent van Gogh to Theo dated September 18, 1888), Greenwich, CT: New York Graphic Society, 1961, 329.

39 "I know of no greater": Franz Kafka, *The Castle*. New York: Schocken Books, 1998.

39 "If you were expecting": Shayla Black, *Wicked Ties* (Wicked Lovers series Book 1). New York: Berkley Publishing Group, 2007, 102.

39 "I keep saying": Dolly Parton, interviewed by Larry King, *Larry King Now*, August 29, 2016, YouTube, https://www.youtube.com/watch?v=Fsq8P9n3hXY.

40 "Eventually you will": Gary Zukav, *The Seat of the Soul*, 25th Anniversary edition. New York: Hay House, 2014, 106.

40 "The supreme happiness": Victor Hugo, *Les Misérables* Volume One. Hertfordshire, UK: Wordsworth Editions Limited, 1994, 112.

41 "Keep love in your heart": Oscar Wilde, *Epigrams: An Anthology*. A. Redman, 1952, 102.

41 "It's my belief": Mark Udall, "I Support Marriage Equality," *Huffington Post*, November 1, 2011, https://www.huffingtonpost.com/entry/senator-mark-udall-i-supp_b_945176.

41 "The more a man judges": Honoré de Balzac, *Part I, Meditation VIII: Of the First Symptoms, aphorism LX*, 1829.

42 "I believe much": Lea T., interviewed by Lisa Capretto, "Transgender Supermodel Lea T. Opens Up About Life After Having Gender Confirmation Surgery," *Huffington Post*, October 28, 2014, https://www.huffpost.com/entry/lea-t-transgender-supermodel-after-surgery_n_6057370.

42 "I want to do": Anaïs Nin, *A Literate Passion: Letters of Anaïs Nin & Henry Miller*. New York: Houghton Mifflin Harcourt, 1987.

42 "There are people": Anne Hathaway, speech, "Love Is a Human Experience," Washington, DC, September 15, 2018, English Central, https://www.englishcentral.com/videodetails/19351.

43 "I am absolutely": Joe Biden, *Meet the Press*, NBC, May 6, 2012, quoted in Matthew Larotonda, "Biden on Gay Marriage: 'Who Do You Love?'" *ABC News*, https://abcnews.go.com/blogs/politics/2012/05/biden-on-gay-marriage-who-do-you-love.

44 "Your friend is the man": Elbert Hubbard, *The Notebook of Elbert Hubbard: Mottos, Epigrams, Short Essays, Passages, Orphic Sayings and Preachments: Coined from a Life of Love, Laughter and Work*. New York: Wm. B Wise & Co, 1927, 112.

44 "Love is the condition": Robert Heinlein, *Stranger in a Strange Land*. New York: Berkley, 1961.

44 "We must love one another": W. H. Auden, *Another Time: Poems*. New York: Random House, 1940.

45 "Being heard is": David W. Augsburger, *Caring Enough to Hear and Be Heard*. Portland, OR: Herald Press, 1982, 12.

45 "Just be you": Naval Ravikant, Twitter, August 14, 2018, https://twitter.com/naval/status/1029274167206600709.

46 "I'm kissing my": Kristen Ellis-Henderson, quoted in Jerry Norwood, "Kristen Henderson of Band Antigone Rising Explains Why She's on the Cover of *Time* Kissing Her Wife," *Time*, April 1, 2013, https://www.out.com/entertainment/popnography/2013/04/01/kiss-time-cover-kristen-henderson-antigone-rising.

46 "I saw with so many": Wade Kach, quoted in Ian Duncan, "Maryland Legislators Pass Gay Marriage Bill," *Los Angeles Times*, February 23, 2012, http://articles.latimes.com/2012/feb/23/nation/la-na-maryland-gay-marriage-20120224.

47 "You don't have": Daniel Radcliffe, interviewed by Larry Carroll, "'Harry Potter' Star Daniel Radcliffe Is 'Passionate About' The Trevor Project," *MTV News*, February 26, 2010, http://www.mtv.com/news/1632811 /harry-potter-star-daniel-radcliffe-is-passionate-about-the-trevor-project/.

48 "As long as": Shonda Rhimes, quoted in Victoria A. Brownworth, "Color, Class & Queers: Shonda Rhimes Re-Writes the TV Landscape to Look Like Us," Pride.com, October 3, 2013, https://www.pride.com /women/2013/10/03/op-ed-color-class-queers-shonda-rhimes-re-writes -tv-landscape-look-us.

48 "I've never had": Joe Manganiello, quoted in Greg Hernandez, *Greg in Hollywood*, "Hunky Joe Manganiello on Why He's an LGBT Ally," September 21, 2014, http://greginhollywood.com/hunky-joe -manganiello-on-why-hes-an-lgbt-ally-im-a-person-who-believes-in -standing-up-for-his-friends-106057.

49 "As a married": Carrie Underwood, quoted in Guy Adams, "Carrie Underwood: US Country Queen Speaks Out for Gay Marriage—But How Will Conservative Fans Take It?" *The Independent*, June 9, 2012, https://www.independent.co.uk/news/world/americas/carrie -underwood-us-country-queen-speaks-out-for-gay-marriage-but-how -will-conservative-fans-take-it-7831956.html.

49 "We will not": Essex Hemphill, *Ceremonies: Prose and Poetry*. Jersey City, NJ: Cleis Press, 2000.

50 "And maybe that's": Charles Blow, "Queer Voices: New York Times Columnist Charles Blow on Revealing He's Bisexual in His New Book," *Huffington Post*, September 26, 2014, https://www.huffpost.com/entry /charles-blow-bisexual_n_5885408/amp.

50 "I say": Christopher Hitchens, *Bill Donohue Debates Christopher Hitchens*, March 23, 2000, YouTube, https://www.youtube.com /watch?v=eQpFTTfs8TI.

50 "It's two people": Janet Jackson, interviewed by Clay Cane, *HX Magazine*, republished on *Janet Love*, February 29, 2008, https://www.janet-love .com/2008/02/29/janet-speaks-to-hx-magazine/.

51 "As far as this body": Rashidi Williams, interviewed by Udoka Okafor, "Exclusive Interview with Rashidi Williams," *Huffington Post*, September 4, 2013, https://www.huffingtonpost.com/udoka-okafor /exclusive-interview-with-rashidi-williams_b_3856754.html.

51 "If anybody can": Will Smith, quoted in Associated Press, "Will Smith Backs Obama's Gay Marriage Stance," *The Washington Times*, May 14, 2012, https://www.washingtontimes.com/news/2012/may/14/will-smith -backs-obama-gay-marriage-stance/.

53 "Just seeing her": Samira Wiley, interviewed by Lisa Butterworth, "'The Handmaid's Tale's' Samira Wiley on Her Wife, Her Wedding, and Being

Out and Proud in Trump's America," *Bust Magazine*, March 21, 2018, https://bust.com/feminism/194349-samira-wiley-cover-sneak-peek.html.

53 "All, everything that I understand": Leo Tolstoy, *War and Peace*. HarperCollins USA, 2018.

53 "Why is it that": Ernest J. Gaines, *A Lesson Before Dying*. New York: Vintage, 1997.

54 "God's love is": Alexya Salvador, quoted in Sarah Marsh and Anett Rios, "Communist-Ruled Cuba Hosts First Transgender Mass," May 7, 2017, https://www.aol.com/article/news/2017/05/09/communist-ruled-cuba-hosts-first-transgender-mass/22076438/.

54 "The mystery and": Del Martin and Phyllis Lyon, *Lesbian/Woman*. New York: Bantam, 1983, 54.

55 "When I was in the military": Epitaph of Leonard P. Matlovich, quoted in Lily Rothman, "How a Closeted Air Force Sergeant Became the Face of Gay Rights," Time.com, September 8, 2015, http://time.com/4019076/40-years-leonard-matlovich/.

55 "So, I love": Paulo Coelho, *The Alchemist*. New York: Harper, 2001.

55 "Married is a magic": Edith Schlain Windsor, "Rally on the Steps of City Hall in Manhattan," speech, Manhattan, NY, February 5, 2009.

56 "Love looks not with the eyes": William Shakespeare, *A Midsummer Night's Dream*. London: Simpkin, Marshall & Co. Hamilton, Adams & Co., 1887.

56 "Love takes off masks": James Baldwin, *The Fire Next Time*. Vintage Books, 1993.

56 "The most important": Morrie Schwartz, quoted in Mitch Albom, *Tuesdays with Morrie*, reprint ed., New York: Broadway, 2002, 52.

57 "I fell in love": F. Scott Fitzgerald, Letter: Cottage Club, Princeton, NJ, to Isabelle Amorous. February 26, 1920.

58 "Love recognizes no": Maya Angelou's Facebook page, January 11, 2013, https://www.facebook.com/MayaAngelou/posts/10151418853254796.

59 "Love many things": Vincent van Gogh, *The Letters of Vincent van Gogh to His Brother, 1872–1886*. London: Constable & Co, 1987.

59 "But I love": Alan Cumming, interviewed by Curtis M. Wong, "Alan Cumming Dishes on Gay Rights, GOP Politics and 'Good Wife' Role at XL Nightclub Benefit Performance," *Huffington Post*, March 19, 2012, https://www.huffingtonpost.com/2012/03/18/alan-cumming-xl-nightclub-performance-gay-rights_n_1360097.html.

Section 3: COURAGE

61 "Act as if": William James, Letter to Helen Keller from *The Correspondence of William James* (Vol. 12, April 1908–August 1910). Charlottesville: University of Virginia Press, 2004.

61 "If anyone is": Beyoncé Knowles, interviewed by Chris Azzopardi, "EXCLUSIVE: Beyoncé Opens Up to Gay Fans," Pridesource.com, July 21, 2011, https://pridesource.com/article/exclusive-beyonc-opens-up-to-gay-fans/.

62 "I am tired": Elliot Page, "Elliot Page Joins HRCF's Time to Thrive Conference," speech, Anaheim, CA, February 14, 2014, https://www.youtube.com/watch?v=1hlCEIUATzg.

62 "I'm well into": Brian Sims, interviewed by David Toussaint, "Brian Sims on Becoming a Gay Sex Symbol, Bears and Why Oprah Should Not Run," Queerty.com, April 29, 2018, https://www.queerty.com/brian-sims-becoming-gay-sexy-symbol-grindr-oprah-not-run-20180429.

63 "Just by being": Danica Roem, quoted in Alana Abramson, "Danica Roem Is Virginia's First Transgender Elected Official," *Time*, November 9, 2017, http://time.com/5016081/danica-roem-2017-elections-virginia-delegate-transgender/.

63 "I tell people": Christine Hallquist, "Vermont Primary Could Pave Way for First Transgender Governor in US," The Guardian.com, August 13, 2018, https://www.theguardian.com/us-news/2018/aug/13/vermont-primary-christine-hallquist-candidate-governor.

64 "We, the people": Barack Obama, "Inaugural Address," January 21, 2013, https://obamawhitehouse.archives.gov/the-press-office/2013/01/21/inaugural-address-president-barack-obama.

65 "I don't want": Susan Allen, quoted in Stephanie Weber, "Minnesota Rep. Susan Allen Is Two-Spirit, a Lesbian, and She Won't Be Assimilated," Slate.com, December 21, 2016, http://www.slate.com/blogs/outward/2016/12/21/susan_allen_minnesota_state_representative_is_lesbian_and_two_spirit_and.html.

65 "All of us": Geena Rocero, "Why I Must Come Out," filmed in Vancouver, British Columbia. TED video, 9:46, March 19, 2014 https://www.ted.com/talks/geena_rocero_why_i_must_come_out?language=en.

65 "Nothing in life": Marie Curie, quoted in Melvin A. Benarde, *Our Precarious Habitat*. New York: W. W. Norton, 1973.

66 "If I wasn't": X González, quoted in Stephanie Marie Anderson, "Emma González Speaks About the Connection Between Her Bisexuality and Her Activism," SBS.com, March 26, 2018, https://www.sbs.com.au/voices/article/emma-gonzalez-speaks-about-the-connection-between-her-bisexuality-and-activism/ak60onayc

66 "With the notion": Lisa Murkowski, "OP-ED: Lisa Murkowski Shares Thoughts on Marriage Equality with Alaskans," June 19, 2013, https://www.murkowski.senate.gov/press/op-ed/op-ed-murkowski-shares-thoughts-on-marriage-equality-with-alaskans.

67 "I would have rather": CeCe McDonald, *Support CeCe McDonald!* (blog).

November 16, 2012, https://supportcece.wordpress.com/2012/11/16/on
-trans-day-of-remembrance-a-proposal/.

67 "When all Americans": Barack Obama, "Obama: Supreme Court Gay
Marriage Ruling Righted a Wrong," Time.com, June 26, 2013, http://
swampland.time.com/2013/06/26/obama-supreme-court-gay-marriage
-ruling-righted-a-wrong/.

67 "I told myself": Malala Yousafzai, *I Am Malala: The Girl Who Stood Up for
Education and Was Shot by the Taliban*. New York: Little, Brown, 2013.

68 "Our understanding of": Debra Kolodny, "From Welcome to Embrace:
Honoring Transgender and Bisexual Jews," *As the Spirit Moves Us*
(blog), January 1, 2013, https://www.asthespiritmovesus.com/from
-welcome-to-embrace-honoring-transgender-and-bisexual-jews-2/.

68 "Of all forms": Bertrand Russell, *The Conquest of Happiness*. New York:
Liveright Publishing Corporation, 1971.

69 "Why be another": Brian Sims, interviewed by David Toussaint,
"Brian Sims on Becoming a Gay Sex Symbol, Bears and Why Oprah
Should Not Run," Queerty.com, April 29, 2018, https://www.queerty
.com/brian-sims-becoming-gay-sexy-symbol-grindr-oprah-not-
run-20180429.

69 "The best way": Robert Frost, "A Servant to Servants," *North of Boston*,
David Nutt, 1914.

69 "They wanted to": CeCe McDonald, quoted in Parker Marie Molloy,
"WATCH: CeCe McDonald Makes First Television Appearance
Following Release from Men's Prison," Advocate.com, January 21,
2014, https://www.advocate.com/politics/transgender/2014/01/21
/watch-cece-mcdonald-makes-first-television-appearance-following.

70 "The greatest test": R. G. Ingersoll, *Great Speeches of Col. R.G. Ingersoll*.
New York: Cosimo Classics, 2009, 63.

70 "I've never been": *bell hooks and Laverne Cox in a Public Dialogue at The
New School*, YouTube, 1:36:09, October 13, 2014, https://www.youtube
.com/watch?v=9oMmZIJijgY.

70 "Providing the healthcare": Rena Janamnuaysook, "The Tangerine
Clinic: Leading the Way on Transgender Health Care," amfar.org,
January 25, 2017, https://www.amfar.org/news/the-tangerine-clinic
-leading-the-way-on-transgender-health-care/.

71 "Be sceptical": Peter Tatchell, quoted in "'Be sceptical and daring':
Peter Tatchell's honorary doctorate acceptance speech," *PinkNews*,
July 26, 2010, https://www.pinknews.co.uk/2010/07/26/be-sceptical
-and-daring-peter-tatchells-honorary-doctorate-acceptance-speech/.

72 "Life shrinks or": Anaïs Nin, quoted in Carol A. Dingle, *Memorable
Quotations: French Writers of the Past*. London: Writers Club Press,
2000, 126.

72 "Equality means more": Barbara Gittings, quoted in Summer Kurtz, "LGBT History Month: How Barbara Gittings Changed the World," medium.com, October 9, 2017, https://medium.com/travelpride/lgbt -history-month-how-barbara-gittings-changed-the-world-e943928d37d3.

72 "I do want": Syd, quoted in Steven J. Horowitz, "The Internet's Syd Wants to Be 'A Pioneer' for Queer Women," billboard.com, June 14, 2018, https://www.billboard.com/articles/news/pride/8460693/syd -the-internet-interview-billboard-pride-2018.

73 "A big part": David Jay, interviewed by Caroline Casper, "The Rumpus Interview with David Jay, Star of the New Documentary, *(A)Sexual*," therumpus.com, August 18, 2011, https://therumpus.net/2011/08/the -rumpus-interview-with-david-jay-star-of-the-new-documentary-asexual/.

74 "I know what": Anne Frank, *The Diary of a Young Girl*. New York: Doubleday, 1967.

74 "In trans women's": Julia Serano, *Whipping Girl: A Transsexual Woman on Sexism and the Scapegoating of Femininity*. Berkeley, CA: Seal Press, 2007.

75 "Some things are": Bruce Springsteen, "A Statement from Bruce Springsteen on North Carolina," brucespringsteen.com, April 8, 2016, http://brucespringsteen.net/news/2016/a-statement-from-bruce -springsteen-on-north-carolina.

75 "Stories make us": Madeleine L'Engle, *The Rock That Is Higher*. New York: Shaw Books, 2002.

76 "I love the": Thomas Paine, "The American Crisis," series of pamphlets, 1776–1783.

77 "I was a": Sylvia Rivera, interviewed by Leslie Feinberg, "Leslie Feinberg Interviews Sylvia Rivera," *Workers World*, 1998, as quoted in Leslie Feinberg, "Street Transvestite Action Revolutionaries: Lavender & Red, Part 73," September 24, 2006, https://www.workers.org/2006 /us/lavender-red-73/.

77 "We need to": Christine Gregoire, quoted in Igor Volsky, "Washington Governor Elated After Introducing Marriage Equality Bill," *Think Progress*, January 4, 2012, https://thinkprogress.org/washington -governor-elated-after-introducing-marriage-equality-bill-i-feel-so -much-better-today-bba0d574d402/.

78 "Don't accept the": Peter Tatchell, quoted in "'Be sceptical and daring': Peter Tatchell's Honorary Doctorate Acceptance Speech," *PinkNews*, July 26, 2010, https://www.pinknews.co.uk/2010/07/26/be-sceptical -and-daring-peter-tatchells-honorary-doctorate-acceptance-speech/.

78 "Our nation's permanent": Bill Clinton, quoted in Jennifer Epstein, "Bill Clinton Backs Gay Marriage Bill," *Politico*, May 5, 2011, https://www .politico.com/story/2011/05/bill-clinton-backs-gay-marriage-bill-054358.

79 "The only tyrant": Mahatma Gandhi, *The Essential Gandhi: An Anthology of His Writings on His Life, Work, and Ideas*. New York: Vintage, 1962.

79 "Now they got": Marsha P. Johnson, *Pay It No Mind—The Life and Times of Marsha P. Johnson*. Dir. Michael Kasino, 2012, YouTube, https://www.youtube.com/watch?v=rjN9W2KstqE/.

80 "If proud Americans": Michelle Obama, "Transcript: Michelle Obama's Convention Speech," npr.org, September 4, 2012, https://www.npr.org/2012/09/04/160578836/transcript-michelle-obamas-convention-speech.

80 "Recognizing our rights": Geraldine Roman, quoted in "Transgender solon lands in US magazine's list of inspiring women," news.abs-cbn.com, October 14, 2016, https://news.abs-cbn.com/life/10/14/16/transgender-solon-lands-in-us-magazines-list-of-inspiring-women.

80 "Have the courage": Steve Jobs, quoted in Alyson Shontell, "Startup Hero Steve Jobs: 'Have the Courage to Follow Your Heart and Your Intuition,'" businessinsider.com, October 6, 2011, https://www.businessinsider.com/with-steve-jobs-death-many-new-entrepreneurs-are-born-2011-10.

81 "There is something": Rev. Al Sharpton, quoted in Ta-Nehisi Coates, "When the Boy Is On, He's On," *The Atlantic*, January 15, 2009, https://www.theatlantic.com/entertainment/archive/2009/01/when-the-boy-is-on-he-apos-s-on/6588/.

81 "I hope the": Adam Eli, interviewed by Joe Rodriguez, "20 Queer Q's with Adam Eli," IntoMore.com, October 21, 2018, https://www.intomore.com/you/20-queer-qs-with-adam-eli.

82 "Do you want a happy little girl": DeShanna Neal, "'Do You Want a Happy Little Girl or a Dead Little Boy?': My Choice as a Mother," Broadly.VICE.com, April 12, 2017, https://broadly.vice.com/en_us/article/8x4qdk/do-you-want-a-happy-little-girl-or-a-dead-little-boy-my-choice-as-a-mother.

82 "When they don't": Marsha P. Johnson, interview in *Out of the Closets: Voices of Gay Liberation*, edited by Karla Jay and Allen Young. New York: New York University Press, 1992.

83 "Don't tell me": Misty Plowright, interviewed by Susan Greene, "Meet Misty Plowright: The Trans, Trekkie Tech Geek Vying to Unseat US Rep. Doug Lamborn," *The Colorado Independent*, July 15, 2016, https://www.coloradoindependent.com/2016/07/15/misty-plowright-doug-lamborn/.

83 "If you don't": Elizabeth Warren, quoted in Tom McKay, "In One Quote, Elizabeth Warren Perfectly Sums Up Why We

Need More Women in Politics," Mic.com, September 23, 2014, https://mic.com/articles/99580/in-one-quote-elizabeth-warren-perfectly -sums-up-why-we-need-more-women-in-politics#.pOOBJGoPi.

83 "If enough people": José Sarria. From Outhistory.org, "Out and Elected in the USA, 1974–2004," http://outhistory.org/exhibits/show/out-and -elected/prelude/jose-sarria.

Section 4: HOPE

85 "I'm seeing changes": Kasha Jacqueline Nabagesera, quoted in Bianca Britton, "Kasha Nabagesera: The Face of Uganda's LGBT Movement," CNN, March 6, 2017, https://www.cnn.com/2017/03/05/africa/her -kasha-jacqueline-nabagesera-lgbt-campaigner/index.html.

85 "What we have": Abhina Aher, interviewed by Julia McCarthy, "All Things Considered," npr.org, April 18, 2014, https://www.npr.org /sections/parallels/2014/04/18/304548675/a-journey-of-pain-and -beauty-on-becoming-transgender-in-india.

85 "At some point": George Clooney, quoted in Katherine Thomson, "George Clooney Slams Prop 8," *Huffington Post*, December 13, 2008, https://www.huffingtonpost.com/2008/11/12/george-clooney-slams -prop_n_143390.html.

86 "There will be": Keisha Michaels, quoted in Claire Warner, "Transhaven LA Is Fighting Trans Homelessness This Holiday Season," *Bustle*, December 23, 2016, https://www.bustle.com/p /transhaven-la-is-fighting-trans-homelessness-this-holiday -season-25914.

86 "The universe has": Miley Cyrus, interviewed by Ramin Setoodeh, "Miley Cyrus on 'The Voice,' Donald Trump and Coming Out," *Variety*, October 11, 2016, https://variety.com/2016/music/features /miley-cyrus-the-voice-donald-trump-vmas-woody-allen-coming-out -pansexual-1201884281/.

87 "It is so important that we": Chelsea Manning, quoted in Diana Tourjée, "'It's Hard to show the World I Exist': Chelsea Manning's Final Plea to Be Seen," Broadly.VICE.com, December 29, 2016, https:// broadly.vice.com/en_us/article/wje8a9/its-hard-to-show-the-world -i-exist-chelsea-mannings-final-plea-to-be-seen.

87 "What keeps me going": Gavin Grimm, "I'm Transgender and Can't Use the Student Bathroom. The Supreme Court Could Change That," *The Washington Post*, October 27, 2016, https://www.washingtonpost .com/opinions/im-transgender-and-cant-use-the-student-bathroom -the-supreme-court-could-change-that/2016/10/27/19d1a3ae-9bc1-11e6 -a0ed-ab0774c1eaa5_story.html?utm_term=.ac9f04a29232.

87 "But I do think": Josh Hutcherson, interviewed by Shana Naomi Krochmal, "Josh Hutcherson Describes His Sexuality," *OUT*, October 11, 2013, https://www.out.com/entertainment/popnography/2013/10/11/josh-hutcherson-describes-his-sexuality-hunger-games.

88 "We have a": Asia Kate Dillon, interviewed by Jeffrey Masters, "Asia Kate Dillon Talks," *Huffington Post*, April 13, 2017, https://www.huffingtonpost.com/entry/asia-kate-dillon-talks-discovering-the-word-non-binary_us_58ef1685e4b0156697224c7a.

88 "If someone says": Jazz Jennings, *Being Jazz*. New York: Penguin Random House, 2016, 179.

88 "I hope that": Heather Purser, interviewed by *Indian Country Today*, "A Foot in Two Worlds: The Battle for Gay Marriage on Tribal Lands," ICT News, April 29, 2015, https://newsmaven.io/indiancountrytoday/archive/a-foot-in-two-worlds-the-battle-for-gay-marriage-on-tribal-lands-keeChabph0uw2i_v1aAIrA.

89 "As we come": Jewelle Gomez, interviewed by Claire Heuchan, "Jewelle Gomez on Writing, Resistance, and Waiting for Giovanni," *AfterEllen*, July 17, 2018, https://www.afterellen.com/entertainment/561869-jewelle-gomez-on-writing-resistance-and-waiting-for-giovanni-interview.

91 "We can only see": Alan Turing, "Computing Machinery and Intelligence," *Mind - A Quarterly Review of Psychology and Philosophy*, vol. 59, no. 239 (1950): 460.

92 "What queer media": Phillip Picardi, interviewed by Max Berlinger, "Phillip Picardi: The Great Gay Hope," *Bonobos*, June 14, 2018, https://milled.com/Bonobos/how-one-man-is-rethinking-the-queer-media-landscape-B8XAl4qV1BcLtvlk.

92 "If you don't": Eric Shinseki, quoted in James Dao and Thom Shanker, "No Longer a Soldier, Shinseki Has a New Mission," *New York Times*, November 10, 2009, https://www.nytimes.com/2009/11/11/us/politics/11vets.html.

92 "This is a": Cecilia Chung, interviewed by Reggie Aqui, "Trans Activist Cecilia Chung Describes Life in San Francisco in 80s," *ABC 7 News San Francisco*, March 2, 2017, https://abc7news.com/society/transgender-activist-cecilia-chung-describes-life-in-sf-in-1980s/1781878/.

93 "I am. I": Arsham Parsi, interviewed by Ceyda Nurtsch, "Rights Are Never Given; We Have to Fight for Them," *Qantara.de*, April 2, 2013, https://en.qantara.de/content/interview-with-lgbt-rights-activist-arsham-parsi-rights-are-never-given-we-have-to-fight-for.

93 "Young people": W. H. Auden, *The Complete Works of W. H. Auden*. Princeton, NJ: Princeton University Press, 2015, 167.

94 "Don't ask yourself": Howard Thurman, as quoted in Gil Bailie, *Violence Unveiled: Humanity at the Crossroads*. New York: Crossroad Publishing Company, 1996, xv.

94 "Having transgender characters": Jazz Jennings, interviewed by Jocelyn McClurg, *USA Today*, August 7, 2016, https://www.usatoday .com/story/life/books/2016/08/07/transgender-teen-fiction-young-adult -books/87262922/.

95 "If you want": Lynn Conway, "Our Travels Through Time," speech, Atlanta, GA, November 28, 2014, http://ai.eecs.umich.edu/people /conway/Memoirs/Talks/OTI/Lynn%27s_OTI_2014_Keynote.html.

95 "All media has": Harish Iyer, interviewed by Sooraj Rajmohan, "All for Love," *The Hindu*, August 7, 2017, https://www.thehindu.com/life -and-style/equal-rights-activist-harish-iyer-tells-the-stories-of-the-lgbt -community-through-his-radio-show-gaydio/article19445448.ece.

96 "I would say": "When Prince William Met Attitude," *Attitude Magazine*, June 15, 2016, https://www.attitude.co.uk/news/world /watch-when-prince-william-met-attitude-289107/.

96 "Every gay and lesbian person": Bob Paris, in Bob Paris-Jackson and Rod Paris-Jackson, *Straight from the Heart*. New York: Grand Central, 1994, 299.

97 "Hell hath no": Sylvia Rivera, quoted in Rob Laczko, "Remembering Sylvia—The Mother of the Riot," *Out in Jersey*, June–July 2010, 4.

98 "Everything about how": Anne Hathaway, *Anne Hathaway Human Rights Campaign Full Speech*, September 15, 2018, YouTube, 11:49, https://www.youtube.com/watch?v=6jmyiCkrXNI.

98 "Just when I think": Hugh Prather, *Notes to Myself*. New York: Bantam Books, 1976, 24.

99 "The only way": Alan Watts, *The Wisdom of Insecurity*. New York: Vintage Books, 2011, 43.

99 "They always say": Andy Warhol, *The Philosophy of Andy Warhol*. New York: Houghton Mifflin Harcourt, 1975.

99 "I'm optimistic about": Phyllis Lyon, quoted in Karman Kregloe, "Veteran LGBT Activist Phyllis Lyon Tells Us 'It Will Be OK,'" *AfterEllen*, May 26, 2009, https://www.afterellen.com/more/51348 -veteran-lgbt-activist-phyllis-lyon-tells-us-it-will-be-ok.

100 "I swear I": Leo Christopher, *Sleeping in Chairs*. Los Angeles: Underwater Mountains, 2015.

100 "If you have": Khader Abu-Seif, interviewed by Kaelyn Forde, "A Gay Muslim-Jewish Couple Living in Israel Has This Powerful Message," *Refinery29*, September 7, 2016, https://www.refinery29.com/en-us /2016/06/114975/gay-muslim-lgbt-pride-orlando-shooting.

101 "Change will not": Barack Obama, "Barack Obama's Feb. 5 Speech" (transcript), *New York Times*, February 5, 2008, https://www.nytimes.com/2008/02/05/us/politics/05text-obama.html.

101 "I wasn't discouraged": Chi Chia-wei, interviewed by Amber Wang, "Labour of Love: One Man's Fight for Gay Marriage in Taiwan," *The Jakarta Post*, May 12, 2017, https://www.thejakartapost.com/life/2017/05/12/labour-of-love-one-mans-fight-for-gay-marriage-in-taiwan.html.

101 "Absolutely! I believe": Shawnee (She King), interviewed by Tiffany Mott-Smith, "She King Brings Her Tour to the United States," *Tagg Magazine*, June 6, 2013, https://taggmagazine.com/catching-shawnee-king/.

102 "Somebody has to": Alice Nkom, interviewed by Cliff Joannou, "A Human Rights Lawyer Describes What It's Like to Defend Cameroon's LGBT People," VICE.com, April 21, 2015, https://www.vice.com/en_us/article/avyzge/we-spoke-to-human-rights-lawyer-alice-nkom-about-defending-cameroon-lgbt-189.

102 "But we aren't": Sage Grace Dolan-Sandrino, OP ED: "I'm a Trans Student, and the Trump Administration Memo Won't Erase Me," *Teen Vogue*, October 23, 2018, https://www.teenvogue.com/story/im-a-trans-student-and-the-trump-administration-memo-wont-erase-me.

102 "I would say the majority": Ian Daniel, interviewed by Jamie Lee Taete, "Ellen Page and Ian Daniel Talk About Documenting Homophobia and Hope Around the World," VICE.com, November 9, 2016, https://www.vice.com/en_us/article/vdbn89/ellen-page-and-ian-daniel-talks-about-documenting-homophobia-and-hope-around-the-world-gaycation.

103 "Whenever I'm asked": Leah Juliett, interviewed by Tembe Denton-Hurst, "Why 1 Survivor of Revenge Porn Wants You to Know It's Not Just a Straight Person's Problem," *POPsugar*, June 24, 2018, https://www.popsugar.com/news/Leah-Juliett-LGBTQ-Pride-Month-Interview-About-Revenge-Porn-44944998.

CONTRIBUTOR LIST

Abhina Aher, b. 1977, Indian transgender activist

Adam Eli, b. 1990, LGBTQ activist and writer

Alan Cumming, b. 1965, Scottish American actor, singer, writer, producer, and activist

Alan Joyce, b. 1966, Australian businessman, CEO of Qantas Airlines

Alan Turing, 1912–1954, mathematician, computer scientist, logician, cryptanalyst, and philosopher

Alan W. Watts, 1917–1973, British American philosopher

Alexander McQueen, 1969–2010, British fashion designer and couturier

Alex Sánchez, Mexican American author of award-winning novels for teens and adults

Alexya Salvador, b. 1980, transgender teacher and reverend in São Paulo, Brazil

Alice Nkom, b. 1945, advocate for decriminalization of homosexuality in Cameroon

Amandla Stenberg, b. 1998, actress

Anaïs Nin, 1903–1977, French American writer

Anderson Cooper, b. 1967, journalist, television personality, and author

André Breton, 1896–1966, French writer, poet, and anti-fascist

André Gide, 1869–1951, French author and winner of the Nobel Prize in Literature

Andy Warhol, 1928–1987, artist, director, and producer

Angel Haze (Raykeea Raeen-Roes Wilson), b. 1991, rapper and singer

Anne Frank, 1929–1945, German-born Jewish diarist

Anne Hathaway, b. 1982, actress and singer

Arnie Kantrowitz, 1940–2022, gay activist, college professor, and writer

Arsham Parsi, b. 1980, Iranian LGBT human rights activist

Asia Kate Dillon, b. 1984, actor

Barack Obama, b. 1961, 44th president of the United States

Barbara De Angelis, b. 1951, relationship consultant, personal growth adviser, and spiritual teacher

Barbara Gittings, 1932–2007, activist for LGBT equality

Bertrand Russell, 1872–1970, British philosopher, logician, mathematician, historian, and political activist

Beyoncé Knowles, b. 1981, singer, songwriter, actress, record producer, and dancer

Bill Clinton, b. 1946, 42nd president of the United States

Blair Imani, b. 1993, African-American Muslim activist

Bob Goddard, 1882–1945, physicist

Bob Paris, b. 1959, Canadian American writer, actor, and civil rights activist

Brené Brown, b. 1965, research professor

Brian Sims, b. 1978, first openly gay elected state legislator in Pennsylvania history

Brittney Griner, b. 1990, professional basketball player

Bruce Springsteen, b. 1949, singer and songwriter

Carrie Underwood, b. 1983, singer, songwriter, and actress

CeCe McDonald, b. 1989, African American bi trans woman and LGBTQ activist

Cecilia Chung, b. 1965, civil rights leader and activist for LGBT rights, HIV/AIDS, health advocacy, and social justice

Charles Blow, b. 1970, journalist, commentator, and op-ed columnist for the *New York Times*

Chaz Bono, b. 1969, writer, musician, and actor

Chelsea Manning, b. 1987, activist and former US Army soldier

Chi Chia-wei, b. 1958, Taiwanese civil rights activist

Christine Gregoire, b. 1947, 22nd governor of the state of Washington

Christine Hallquist, b. 1956, first openly transgender major party nominee for governor in the United States

Christopher Hitchens, 1949–2011, British American writer and social critic

Courtney Act, b. 1982, Australian drag queen, pop singer, entertainer, and reality TV personality

Dan Coppersmith, b. 1950, cryptographer and mathematician

Danica Roem, b. 1984, journalist, politician, and first openly transgender person elected to the Virginia General Assembly

Daniel Radcliffe, b. 1989, English actor and producer

David Jay, b. 1982, asexual activist

David W. Augsburger, b. 1938, American Anabaptist and writer

Debby Boone, b. 1956, American singer, author, and actress

Debra Kolodny, bisexual rights activist and congregational rabbi

DeShanna Neal, community organizer for families of trans youth and the first non-binary elected state legislator in Delaware history

Dolly Parton, b. 1946, country singer, songwriter, instrumentalist, actress, author, and philanthropist

E. M. Forster, 1879–1970, English novelist, short story writer, essayist, and librettist

Edith Schlain Windsor, 1929–2017, LGBT rights activist and technology manager at IBM

Edward Estlin Cummings, 1894–1962, poet, painter, essayist, author, and playwright

Edwin Elliot, 1851–1937, mathematician

Elbert Hubbard, 1856–1915, writer and philosopher

Eleanor Roosevelt, 1884–1962, political figure, diplomat, and activist

Elizabeth Warren, b. 1949, US senator from Massachusetts

Ellen DeGeneres, b. 1958, comedian, television host, actress, writer, producer, and LGBT activist

Elliot Page, b. 1987, Canadian actor, producer, and activist

Elton John, b. 1947, English singer, pianist, and composer

Eric Shinseki, b. 1942, retired US Army general

Ernest J. Gaines, b. 1933–2019, African American author

Essex Hemphill, 1957–1995, openly gay American poet and activist

Evan Rachel Wood, b. 1987, actress, model, and musician

F. Scott Fitzgerald, 1896–1940, writer

Franz Kafka, 1883–1924, German-speaking Bohemian Jewish novelist

Gary Zukav, b. 1942, author and spiritual teacher

Gavin Grimm, transgender activist

Geena Rocero, b. 1983, Filipino American supermodel, speaker, and transgender advocate

George Bernard Shaw, 1856–1950, Irish playwright, critic, and political activist

George Clooney, b. 1961, actor, filmmaker, and businessman

George Eliot, 1819–1880, writer of the Victorian era

Geraldine Roman, b. 1967, Filipino journalist and politician

Hanne Gaby Odiele, b. 1988, Belgian model, born intersex

Hari Nef, b. 1992, actress, model, and writer

Harish Iyer, b. 1979, activist

Harvey Milk, 1930–1978, politician and first openly gay elected official in the history of California

Heather Purser, LGBT advocate, diver, and member of Suquamish tribe in Seattle, Washington

Helen Keller, 1880–1968, author, political activist, and lecturer

Henry Miller, 1891–1980, writer

Honoré de Balzac, 1799–1850, French novelist and playwright

Howard Thurman, 1899–1981, African American author, philosopher, theologian, educator, and civil rights leader

Hugh Prather, 1938–2010, self-help writer, lay minister and counselor

Ian Daniel, host of documentary series *Gaycation*

James Baldwin, 1924–1987, writer and activist

Janelle Monaé, b. 1985, singer, songwriter, actress, and producer

Janet Jackson, b. 1966, singer, actress, and dancer

Janet Mock, b. 1983, writer, television host, director, producer, and transgender rights activist

Jazz Jennings, b. 2000, YouTube personality, spokesmodel, and LGBT rights activist

Jennifer Hudson, b. 1981, singer and actress

Jewelle Gomez, b. 1948, writer

Jim Morrison, 1943–1971, singer, songwriter, and poet

Joe Biden, b. 1942, 46th president of the United States

Joe Manganiello, b. 1976, actor

John Winston Ono Lennon, 1940–1980, English singer, songwriter, and peace activist who co-founded the Beatles

Jonathan Van Ness, b. 1987, hairdresser, podcaster, and television personality

José Sarria, 1922–2013, political activist and first openly gay candidate for public office in the United States

Josh Hutcherson, b. 1992, actor and producer

Julia Serano, b. 1967, writer, spoken-word performer, trans-bi activist, and biologist

Karamo Brown, b. 1980, television host, reality television personality, and activist

Kasha Nabagesera, b. 1980, Ugandan LGBT rights activist

Keisha Michaels, pediatrician and parent of transgender teenage girl

Khader Abu-Seif, gay Palestinian Muslim featured in the documentary film *Oriented*

Kristen Ellis-Henderson, b. c. 1988, guitarist and songwriter for Antigone Rising, writer, and LGBT activist

Lady Gaga, b. 1986, singer, songwriter, and actress

Lani Ka'ahumanu, b. 1943, bisexual and feminist writer and activist

Laverne Cox, b. 1972, American actress and LGBT advocate

Leah Juliett, b. 1997, LGBTQ+ speaker, writer, performer, and activist

Lea T, b. 1981, Brazilian-born, Italian-raised transgender fashion model

Lena Waithe, b. 1984, screenwriter, producer, and actress

Leo Tolstoy, 1828–1910, Russian writer

Lisa Murkowski, b. 1957, US senator from Alaska

Loretta Young, 1913–2000, actress

Lynn Conway, b. 1938, computer scientist, electrical engineer, inventor, and transgender activist

Mabel Hampton, 1902–1989, lesbian activist, dancer during the Harlem Renaissance, and philanthropist for both Black and lesbian/gay organizations

Madeleine L'Engle, 1918–2007, writer of young adult fiction

Mae West, 1893–1980, actress, singer, playwright, screenwriter, and comedian

Mahatma Gandhi, 1869–1948, Indian activist

Malala Yousafzai, b. 1997, Pakistani activist for female education and the youngest Nobel Prize laureate

Marianne Williamson, b. 1952, spiritual teacher, author, lecturer, entrepreneur, and activist

Marie Curie, 1867–1934, physicist and chemist, first woman to win a Nobel Prize

Mark Udall, b. 1950, former US senator from Colorado

Marsha P. Johnson, 1945–1992, gay liberation activist and self-identified drag queen

Mary Dunbar, 1906–1960, British artist, illustrator, and teacher

Maya Angelou, 1928–2014, poet, singer, memoirist, and civil rights activist

Meg Medina, Cuban American writer of young adult fiction

Michelle Obama, b. 1964, writer, lawyer, and former First Lady of the United States

Miley Cyrus, b. 1992, singer, songwriter, and actress

Misty Plowright, b. 1983, one of the first two openly transgender people in the United States to be a candidate for a major political party for a national office

Morrie Schwartz, 1916–1995, sociology professor and author

Naval Ravikant, b. 1974, entrepreneur and founder of AngelList

Neil Patrick Harris, b. 1973, American actor, writer, producer, magician, and singer

Oscar Wilde, 1854–1900, Irish poet and playwright

Paulo Coelho, b. 1947, Brazilian lyricist and novelist

Paul Valéry, 1871–1945, French writer and philosopher

Phillip Picardi, b. 1991, journalist and editor-in-chief of *Out* magazine

Phyllis Lyon (1924–2020) and Del Martin (1921–2008), feminist and gay rights activists

Portia de Rossi, b. 1973, Australian American model, philanthropist, and actress

Prince William, b. 1982, member of the British royal family

R. G. Ingersoll, 1833–1899, writer and orator

Ralph Waldo Emerson, 1803–1882, essayist and poet

Rashidi Williams, social entrepreneur, HIV and sexual health educator, and human rights defender

Rena Janamnuaysook, Thai transgender advocate for health and human rights

Rev. Al Sharpton, b. 1954, civil rights activist, Baptist minister, and talk show host

Rita Mae Brown, b. 1944, writer, activist, and feminist

Robert Frost, 1874–1963, poet

Robert Heinlein, 1907–1988, writer, aeronautical engineer, and retired Naval officer

Robert Morley, 1908–1992, English actor

Robert Wolf Eagle, member of the Comanche Nation

Robyn Ochs, b. 1958, bisexual activist

Rumi, 1207–1273, Persian poet, jurist, Islamic scholar, and theologian

RuPaul, b. 1960, drag queen, actor, model, singer, songwriter, and television personality

Sage Grace Dolan-Sandrino, b. 2000, trans LGBTQ activist

Samira Wiley, b. 1987, American actress and model

Schuyler Bailar, b. 1996, first openly transgender NCAA Division I swimmer

Shamina Singh, president of the Center for Inclusive Growth at Mastercard

Shawnee (She King), Canadian vocalist and performer

Shonda Rhimes, b. 1970, television producer and author

Sir Ian McKellen, b. 1939, English stage and screen actor

Sophocles, 497–406 BCE, ancient Greek playwright

Steve Jobs, 1955–2011, business magnate and investor, former CEO and co-founder of Apple

Susan Allen, b. 1963, first Native American woman to serve in the Minnesota Legislature and the first openly lesbian Native American to win election to a state legislature

Syd, b. 1992, singer, songwriter, DJ, record producer, and audio engineer

Sylvia Rivera, 1951–2002, Latina American gay liberation and transgender rights activist

Tammy Baldwin, b. 1962, first openly gay woman elected to Congress

Tan France, b. 1983, English fashion designer and television personality

Tegan Quin, b. 1980, Canadian indie pop musician and songwriter

Thaddeus Golas, 1924–1997, writer and author of *The Lazy Man's Guide to Enlightenment*

Thomas Paine, 1737–1809, political activist, philosopher, and revolutionary

Tim Cook, b. 1960, CEO of Apple Inc.

Tom Nestor, founder of All Under One Roof (safe space for LGBT youth in rural Idaho)

Tyra Banks, b. 1973, television personality, producer, businesswoman, actress, author, and model

Victor Hugo, 1802–1885, French writer of the Romantic movement

Vincent van Gogh, 1853–1890, Dutch Post-Impressionist painter

W. H. Auden, 1907–1973, English American poet

Wade Kach, b. 1947, politician

Walt Whitman, 1819–1892, poet, essayist, and journalist

William James, 1842–1910, philosopher and psychologist

William Shakespeare, 1564–1616, English poet, playwright, and actor

Will Smith, b. 1968, actor and rapper

Winston Churchill, 1874–1965, British politician, army officer, and writer

X González, b. 1999, activist and advocate for gun control

Zelda Fitzgerald, 1900–1948, American socialite, novelist, painter, and wife of author F. Scott Fitzgerald